The Master of the Cube

Mike Newlyn

chipmunkapublishing
the mental health publisher

All rights reserved, no part of this publication may be reproduced by any means, electronic, mechanical photocopying, documentary, film or in any other format without prior written permission of the publisher.

>Published by
>Chipmunkapublishing
>PO Box 6872
>Brentwood
>Essex CM13 1ZT
>United Kingdom

http://www.chipmunkapublishing.com

Copyright © Mike Newlyn 2011

Edited by Aleks Lech

Chipmunkapublishing gratefully acknowledge the support of Arts Council England.

The Master of the Cube

Michael Newlyn was born in the city of Winchester in 1973 and lives in a small village in Hampshire called Bishops Waltham. He has lived there most of his life and attended infants school in Swanmore. Michael is also an artist using pencils ink and also develops digital art and media. He has a passion of music too, writing deep from the heart about life experiences and about his experiences with mental illness. He suffers from mental health issues as like his Father who also had mental illness difficulties. He has had experiences of hospital and he also cared for his Father as he had Huntingtons disease. His passion is animals; creativity, music and his fascination with the universe and believing people should be treated fairly at all times...

Mike Newlyn

The Master of the Cube

Mike Newlyn

The Master of the Cube

For Marilyn...

Mike Newlyn

The Master of the Cube

To my Father, David, with love and thanks
1949-2002

Mike Newlyn

The Master of the Cube

Contents

1) Brave Peter

2) The man with two brains

3) Ulysses

4) The master of the cube

5) The tragic Hollywood love affair

Mike Newlyn

The Master of the Cube

Mike Newlyn

BRAVE PETER

During the long Winter of 1978, Britain was undergoing punishment, left out in the cold after the widespread strikes of the trade Unions. I was living in Southampton, right on the corner of 'London Road', with Elaine, my pregnant fiancée who was eight months gone at the time!

The heavy rain was constantly lashing across the empty street leaving coloured liquid transparent puddles of oil rushing towards the drains. 'My name is Joshua by the way, I am currently working in an electrical store on Bank Street, Sago. Their corporate name is Technologies; they are a small company dealing in new and used televisions, cookers and hi-fi equipment. I don't like working there, but the money pays the bills and gets food on the table.'

Elaine was at home, just finishing cooking the evening meal for Joshua and she was looking forward to him coming home. The rain was really lashing down now and she could hear the comforting splatters on the windows as the wind lashed the front porch, tossing a bucket into the street!

Elaine cooked really nice meals. She once worked as a dinner lady at the local school cooking for bunches of screaming kids. She chuckled to herself as she remembered how the children would always sit on the edge of their seats, plates at the ready, desperate for the magic word.. 'Seconds!!'

Then fifty fighting kids would bundle towards the canteen all at once!! There was one particular boy whom she found very odd, 'William' he was so funny, she thought. William would always try to balance his food on his fork, he never attempted or used a fork in the correct way; did his parents not show him the proper way to do it? Was he just inquisitive? Crazy even!!

    I arrived home. I was drenched from head to toe, my anorak was saturated from the November storms and I was looking forward to seeing Elaine, sitting down and having some tea! I opened the front door and slammed it shut abruptly, shielding myself from the violent winds.
'Elaine, I'm back' I shouted through to the kitchen, Elaine came through and gave me a kiss.
'God Josh, your drenched, better get out of those wet clothes!' she said, concerned.
 'Sure' I replied, and took off my trousers.

I placed all my wet clothes on the radiators throughout the house and changed into something more comfortable. Elaine turned on the telly and it was 'Top of the Pops', 'Quo were on tonight' I thought, excited! I am really into the Quo, I have followed them since the early seventies with songs such as 'In my Chair' and they are of course the unstoppable 'Frantic Four'. Then I chuckled to myself.

    Elaine brought in my tea as I sat in the

The Master of the Cube

armchair. I watched and waited for the Quo to come on. Elaine had cooked me ham and cheese toasted sandwiches, which was my favourite. I took the plate in my hands.

'Thanks Elaine' I said with a look of appreciation.
'Eat up dear' said Elaine, smiling.

I tucked in. Elaine sat in the armchair opposite and watched telly with me. Finally the Quo came on. 'Great!!' I thought. The song title came up on the screen 'Mystery song'. I must admit, I had not heard their new single yet, so I was really excited. Rick Parfitt was fronting the song, I noticed. Rick's shirt was unbuttoned, wide open with the air billowing through his clothes and his blond hair blowing outwards.

'What a cool guy!' I said to Elaine with a grin.
'Yes, he reminds me of an angel!' replied Elaine with a cheeky look.

The song was great, lots of pumping guitar energy, and it had sprung to mind that the song was actually about a prostitute! - Which I thought was rather a cool idea.
We were happily watching telly when suddenly Elaine let out an almighty yelp!

'Ah!' gasped Elaine.
'What the hell is wrong?' I asked, concerned.
I looked down at the carpet and saw the floor was wet.

'My water's have broken!' gasped Elaine.
I rushed to her aid and checked to see if she was all right.

'What shall I do?' I asked in a panicked tone.
'Quick, get to the phone, I think it's started!!' Elaine shouted.
I rushed to the phone still shaking and picked up the receiver. I dialled nine nine nine and a lady answered.

'Which emergency service do you require?' she asked.
'Ambulance,' I replied.
'My fiancee has gone into labour!' I said breathlessly.
'3 London Road, Southampton' I stated.
'Just keep calm, we will send an ambulance out to you right away!!' the woman said.

I promptly put down the receiver and rushed over to Elaine.
'They are on their way, just sit tight, they will be here soon!' I said to Elaine, arching my arm over her shaking shoulder.

The ambulance arrived in good time but it seemed like hours had passed. There was a loud rap at the door and I rushed out and let the two men in. They were very big built men, one was dark and the other had red hair with a freckled face and a touch of acne.
'Hello, where is she?' said the dark one.
'She's in the front room, follow me' I said as I

The Master of the Cube

rushed into the front room.

The two men had a wheelchair ready for Elaine, and blankets to wrap her up warm in the cold storms of November. They helped Elaine into the chair and gave her oxygen to help her breathe, as the contractions had started.

'She is a little early, three weeks in fact!' I said concerned to the man with the red hair. 'Don't worry, I am sure it will be all fine' he said compassionately as we boarded the ambulance.
Inside the dark man closed the doors of the ambulance and the other spotty man stayed in the back and checked Elaine's blood pressure and well being.
'Don't worry Elaine; we will soon be there!' I said calmly holding Elaine's hand tightly.
'I'm scared!' said Elaine in a trembling voice.
'You will be fine Miss Perkins' said the red haired man scratching his nose.

We soon reached the hospital and the wind was still really gusty. I could hear it crashing against the side of the ambulance, rattling the doors with a clatter, clatter sound and rocking the cradle. The red haired man got up, opened the back doors and got the wheel chair ready for Elaine to go to the maternity part of the hospital I presumed, still holding Elaine's hand tight. Elaine was still breathing heavily and holding her stomach area with a bloated rosy look in cheeks. I was really worried and I thought at one point, 'God, how I could use some of that oxygen!' but came to the conclusion it was totally absurd and childish.

Elaine sat in the wheel chair still looking very upset and tired and as we proceeded to the doors of the hospital, suddenly Elaine screeched out again and squeezed my hand tight, bloody tight in fact, so bloody tight I yelled out as well!!
'Did that hurt Josh?', said Elaine,
'Yes' I replied, 'NOW YOU KNOW WHAT IT BLOODY FEELS LIKE!!!!!' said Elaine aggressively, which I must admit was a real shock to me.
'Is that natural?' I asked the man.
'Yes, some women can be aggressive in childbirth, so don't be alarmed!!' said the man with a smile.
'This is beginning to become a very worrying and stressful situation! I have got be strong!' I thought as we walked through the doors of the hospital.

Inside the hospital was what I had expected. It was very busy, with lots of doctors and nurses going about their duties. A tall dark man walked towards us.
'Hello, Dr. Winter, follow me, I'll fetch the midwife for you' said the doctor in a kind voice as we followed him into an adjacent corridor.
The ambulance men had gone by this point and my nervous anxious state hadn't really got any better and I wasn't prepared for what happened next.

Dr. Winter opened the two doors leading into the delivery room and Elaine and I followed closely behind, as I pushed the wheelchair towards the bedside. Inside the delivery room were lots of breathing apparatus, and of course the midwife.

The Master of the Cube

She was a jolly sort of lady, coloured, with an insane over exaggerated giggle that rippled through my brains. 'Who was this woman? She seemed too potty to deliver a baby let alone be a midwife' I felt strongly.
'Hello Elaine darling I'm Roxy, don't worry everything will be fine!' said the midwife in a jolly tone.

I studied 'Roxy' more closely; she was round, big, and had an amazing beaming smile... 'I guess the sort of person you would expect to see on those daytime cookery programs.' I thought to myself quietly. Even though she was clearly mad, she had a very gentle nature about her, so I decided to put my trust in her and longed to have a baby girl or bouncing boy. We were both hoping it would be a boy, we had a name for him, 'Peter' and 'Elizabeth' if it happened to be a girl, but we were really set on a little boy.

The next moment I can't recall. My anxiety reached breaking point. I suffer from a disorder known as 'GAD' generalised anxiety disorder, which makes every day hard to cope with. I suddenly began to feel a tightening sensation around my neck, also felt dizzy and then nothing…just nothing…just black.

I came to around about six. What on earth had happened? Where was I? I looked about the room; I could see nurses outside talking and going about their duties. I quickly sat up. I felt a little dizzy. 'What was going on?' I thought to myself, bemused.

I got off the leather couch and proceeded to the door. I quickly turned the handle and opened the door; the bright lights dazzled my eyes as I squinted to see. I was immediately approached by a man in a white jacket. 'Mr Oslow?' said the man.
'Yes' I replied.
'I think you better follow me into my office' said the man calmly, but I knew something was wrong!

The doctor took me into his office and closed to door. 'Take a seat...I'm afraid I have some very sad news!' he said. 'Oh no, what?' I said, worried.
'Miss Perkin's sadly passed away a few hours ago' he said.
'What!' I said, trembling with disbelief, holding my hands in my head.
'No' I said.
'God, the baby' I thought.
'What about the baby?' I said with tears in my eyes.
'Your son is fine, Mr Oslow, he is a beautiful baby boy' he said compassionately.
'There was a complication during birth, we did everything we could, I'm really sorry' said the doctor.
'I knew it!!' I shouted in a rage.
'It was that darn Roxy!!' I screamed.
'Calm down Mr Oslow, I know you're upset, but...' He hesitated.
'It's all her fault,' I said, as I helplessly slid down the door in absolute remorse.
The doctor came over and held me in his arms, as I wept hopelessly like a child.

The Master of the Cube

Some five years later…

Peter woke, sat up, rubbed his eyes from the sleepy dust as his dad always called it and put on his Batman dressing gown. Peter loved his dad but never knew his mother 'Elaine'. She died in childbirth having him. His dad would often sit at the kitchen table with the light off, just sobbing to himself, yearning for Elaine to return but she never came, listening to Elaine's favourite song, 'Dancing Queen' by Abba.

Peter rushed downstairs to be with his dad at breakfast time as he loved to do every morning.
'Hi mush!' I said to my chirpy faced little boy.
Peter was a cheeky little boy with spiked blond hair and NHS glasses. The only problem was people picked on Peter for his tired eye which infuriated me, and they very nastily broke his glasses. I had already been to see the headmaster twice with Peter complaining about bullying. I was bullied at school too, so I know how soul destroying it can be and I loved my little boy.
'Want some Ready brek son?' I asked Peter.
'Yes' Peter nodded.
'And will I glow, Daddy?' asked Peter.
'Yes, just like on telly' I said with a grin. I have always made Peter believe he would glow like a candle, just like on the TV ad, as his gran walked him to school on a winters morning.

'Better not be late, I'll drop you off at gran's house soon, eat up and get ready for school' I said.
'OK,' Peter replied, eating his Ready brek.

Peter was now four. I wanted his fifth birthday to be special, really special, and I had bought Peter a really nice bmx for his special day which he asked for. He was also a big fan of American football, even though I thought he was rather young to like such a violent game. He wanted to watch the 1982 super bowl in January. It would be on too late though, but I will let him see it I suppose.

I dropped Peter off at Mum's and headed off to work, I had another day in the electrical shop on Bank Street, and I also had to fix two computers today, ZX81. I am planning to buy Peter a ZX81 soon, but they are a whopping ninety nine pounds. I just could not afford it at the moment, with the Peter's bmx and everything.

Peter walked into his gran's kitchen and gave her a big hug before school.
'Have you got your lunch box?' asked Gran.
'Yes' replied Peter.
'Better get you off to school Peter, you have assembly this morning!' said Gran with a smile.
Peter liked assembly; it was his chance to see Louise, a girl he really liked. She was a beautiful girl in Peter's eyes, and he dared not tell his dad through fear of embarrassment and teasing from other pupils.

Peter lined up for assembly in the dining area at school with his friends, Mick, Tim and Paul. He liked them a lot because they didn't tease him like others did. 'Conkers' said Tim with bizarre look on his face.

The Master of the Cube

'What?' replied Peter.

'Conkers later at break time, yes, we will play conkers!' said Tim with a giggle.

'Tim, you can't play conkers! You are silly, it's silly game!' said Paul, shoving his fingers in his mouth.

The odd thing about Paul was that he always shoved his fingers in his mouth as well as sucking his thumb, which looked really comical as he stood there with his security blanket. They all shuffled into assembly with Mr Tumlow the head looking over at them with a stern look about him. Mr Tumlow was a tall man, with bi-focal specs which sat on the end of his big nose and his wig of course. 'Why is he called Mr Tumlow? Has he got a low tummy or something?' Peter thought, bemused and bewildered.

Peter sat with his mates and waited secretly for Louise to arrive from another class. He finally spotted her. She had long blonde hair which shone in the summer sun, shimmering beautiful tints of delight upon Peter's bulging eyes. Peter often thought of her. He was dead sure she liked him too, from the way she would always try and look round at him in assembly and at playtime. Mr Tumlow walked on to the stage and stood at the lectern and placed his books upon it, straightening his specs on the end of his nose.

'Welcome pupils, I hope you are all well and enjoying yourselves' he said, peering down the end of nose.

He often tended to go boss eyed which made Peter want to laugh.

As the headmaster waffled on Peter was not really listening. He was more interested in Louise, waiting for that moment, a quick glance into her eyes, those beautiful eyes. Louise always made the effort too to look out for Peter, and would look at him like crazy at the end of the assembly which he always looked forward to.

I arrived at the school gates waiting for Peter. I always looked forward to seeing him after school; Peter lighting up and laughing at the lollypop lady in her outfit. I had been troubled by chest pain today but came to the conclusion it was indigestion from the fried breakfast I had eaten that morning so thought not much more of it.
Peter hugged me, and got in the front of the car.
'Put your seat belt on, Peter' I said, being safe, as Peter pulled on his belt with a lollypop in his mouth.

'There it goes again! Chest pain' I thought.
'No, indigestion' I muttered to myself.
We soon arrived home. Peter rushed up into his bedroom to watch 'Renta Ghost', while I walked into the kitchen to put the tea on, still troubled by chest pain.

Peter put on his TV, tuned into his favourite, 'Renta Ghost' and settled down on his bed sucking his lollypop, giggling to himself at the same time. Suddenly Peter heard an almighty crash downstairs in the kitchen!
'Is daddy angry?' thought Peter, alarmed, and rushed downstairs.
Peter rushed into the kitchen and to his horror saw

his dad slumped up against the washing machine holding his chest.

'What's wrong Daddy?' said Peter with tears in his eyes, but his dad did not answer and screwed his face up in pain like he was seriously constipated or something. Peter rushed to the phone.

'I have to help daddy' he thought, and dialled nine nine nine.

Nervously and naively he told the woman about his daddy. The woman told Peter he was a good boy and to wait with his dad just a little longer, till someone came around.

The ambulance arrived in a few minutes. Peter opened the door and let them in, and they rushed into the kitchen and found me on the floor. They knew straight away that I had suffered a heart attack and rushed me to hospital with Peter...

One week later...

'Peter, you are a very brave boy!' said Mr Tumlow with a rosette in his hands with a gold number in the centre. I gave Peter a big hug while telling him I loved him and thanked him for saving my life. Peter was absolutely delighted to receive a special rosette on his birthday, plus a super duper bmx, and smiled pleasantly at Mr Tumlow as Louise watched her hero. Mr Tumlow awarded the rosette with a large gold 1st in the middle to Peter and the whole of assembly clapped and cheered for my little brave Peter...

THE MAN WITH TWO BRAINS

David watched the snow flakes fall on the grounds of the Hospital, like little white petals from an abandoned flower or as if a pillow had been aggressively torn apart releasing its feathers into the sky. He sat quietly, muddled and confused in his world, watching the sky, trying to shut out his inner voice. Screams could be heard in the ward, bangs and crashes would echo through the corridors and then a ghostly silence would fall. David was my father, a very special father, he would always make sure I had a decent cooked breakfast every morning, and he was the most loving father anyone could wish to have. He protected me when I was little after the cruel treatment from my mother and her deranged boyfriend 'Peter' who was just a blatantly evil man!

The truth is that my father had had just about enough, affected by severe mental illness, and Huntington's disease on top of that. 'Why him? Why not someone else? An evil man like Peter!' I

The Master of the Cube

thought. My mother never accepted my father and me. All I wanted was to be loved by my mother but she didn't know how, or just didn't want to. I was taken from my mother in 1978, when I was four, under the child protection order and I was placed into care where I met Kerry. I remember Kerry, not too well though, it was many years ago. One memory I do have is that she was a kind girl, and very grown up for her age. I remember when Kerry was stung on the foot by a bee, she was crying, but I also was weeping for another reason, which I just can't recall now.

David sat at the breakfast table; Brian was sat adjacent on the other table as screams could be heard from further down the ward. The ward had an odd name, 'Gail Braith'. It was a locked, secure ward and rather run down I must say, but the most used of the three remaining wards of the hospital.

'Dave! You alright?' Brian called across the tables, but David didn't answer.
'Dave! Mate!' Still David was not listening, he was wrapped up in his own world, a psychotic world where everyone and everything had a meaning.
I liked Brian, I got on well with him, and he was a nice young man who looked out for my father.
David sat quietly staring at his plate as he didn't feel like eating any food. He was just waiting patiently for me, Michael.

I sat on the little green number 7 bus as I always did on a Saturday to see my dad at the hospital; I looked forward to the bus stopping at the bottom of

'Gravel hill'. A very nice, blonde and pleasant girl would get on the bus and she would smile at me, which was really nice on a bright summer afternoon. The bus arrived at the hospital, and stopped by the little road outside the front of the entrance. I said 'thank you' to the driver, and stepped out in the midday sun. The birds were singing loving little chirps of song throughout the grounds as the light breeze blew through my hair. This felt cool and refreshing.

I walked around the grounds for a moment and as I did so I noticed a man I had seen before. He was constantly walking up and down in a bizarre fashion humming to himself as he did this. I studied and watched him in his own little world; he did not really notice me or acknowledge me even, as he was far away in cuckoo land. The man was of dark complexion, he had an Indian look about him and he wore dark brown clothes, which did not really suit him!

I decided to leave the man on his own little mission and go to 'Gail Braith'. I had to ring the bell on the door once I was there. I took a deep breath as I rung the bell and a large built man with a walky-talky unlocked and opened the doors to the rundown Gail Braith. I walked in. All was calm, and I walked into the main smoking area which had a little round wooden table with magazines strewn upon it. My dad was sat there quietly. He did not look too happy though, he had a haunted ghostly perplexed look on his face, and he was quite withdrawn on that day. I sat down next to him.

The Master of the Cube

There were a few other people sat around his table, a man whom I had not seen before and a young woman. 'Hello dad!' I said; no answer. 'Are you alright?' I said concerned; still no answer. The man on the other chair began to speak...

'Sorry, what's your name?' he asked me in an apologetic tone.
'Mike' I replied, glancing at the young woman sat opposite.
'Hi, I'm Mat' he said in a kindly voice, as we shook hands.
'What do you do?' asked Mat.
'Oh, I am an artist and musician!' I said.
'Oh really, what do you play?' he asked, intrigued.
'The guitar and piano. I've got some pictures in my portfolio!' I said.
'Show us!' he said in a friendly tone.

I unzipped my portfolio and I took out my masterpieces. Immediately the young woman opposite intervened, wanting to see what I had. She was a pretty young thing, probably about twenty or so and she had a blonde bobbed haircut. She as I could tell was a trainee nurse or something.

'God, I like these' she said.
'Thank you' I replied with a smile of appreciation.
'How do you do it?' asked Mat curiously.
'With inks and an airbrush' I replied.

During the conversation I had realised that I had not shown my father much attention and turned to

him with a smile. Immediately he sprung into life, with a big bang!
His eyes began to bulge, bulge with anger!

'YOU COME DOWN HERE, NICK MY FLAT, AND LEAVE ME IN THIS FUCKING PLACE! I'M COMING HOME WHETHER YOU LIKE IT OR NOT!' he shouted whilst aggressively prodding me in the arm.
I found this very upsetting and as he kept pounding me, with verbal abuse, I hid my face in my hands, and then I snapped!

He pushed me too far this time! I stood up and as he stood I pushed him back down on the seat. His face went bright red and he was like a wild animal. 'MICHAEL!' he shouted. 'MICHAEL, COME HERE!' he said as I made a run for it. He chased me like I was a rabbit and he was the wild fox! I was really scared, he had such a wild look on his face and he was also on 'section 3'. I quickly turned the corner of the ward by the boxing bag, and with all the shouting and commotion the staff bundled out of the kitchen and then very aggressively pinned him to the floor.

My dad was screaming, yelling, fighting, kicking his legs and arms. I felt tears come to my eyes as I stood there and watched as the male nurses sedated him with a needle. I was then joined by two female nurses, and as I sat down on a chair near the boxing bag a dark haired lady knelt down in front of me. They told me it was probably better if I go home as my father was very ill. I left

The Master of the Cube

the hospital and as I walked past the outside the window I heard my dad scream out again in a rage!

Sadly Huntington's disease is in our family. My father was diagnosed after week long tests in the Neurology part of the Southampton General Hospital. The disease was in its infancy in the beginning and only my family and I could see the early signs. HD is a hereditary gradual degeneration of the nervous system and brain cells, and I was not sure of what my future would hold because I had not had the test for the faulty gene. I went home on the bus, which I always hated because of the distress in visiting my father, but it was not always like this. My Father was a good man, he took care of me and he loved me as his only son, I was everything to him, and he also meant a lot to me despite everything. My father was also very protective of me and he suddenly hit the roof when he found out I was being bullied at school!

'Oslow…yes, smart arse Oslow.' How I hated that guy, he was a nothing but a bully and so was his pathetic brother. They both made my childhood hell; bullies, how I hate bullies! I can remember Oslow; curly dark hair, older than me, skinny and a little weasel as far as I was concerned! They were so nasty to me; they called me names, made fun of me and broke my glasses! I did not like how one minute they were my friends and next my enemies, why? I'll never forget the years of hell they caused me and I feel for the children who suffered like I did.

David sat in the smoking area. He had been transferred to another ward, 'New Oaks', shortly after his second suicide attempt. He would often escape from the hospital, and he had on his mind how he had to free himself from this prison. David sat not really taking in his surroundings, but he had Rose to talk to on the ward. Rose was nice, very friendly, she had burning red hair and a limp due to what I believe was her false leg. I don't really know how she lost her leg, I never thought to ask her really. David's whole world surrounded him, the hospital, that hospital which he hated and feared. He wanted to be home, how he wanted to be at home with Michael. The nurses said my father had made progress and he was adjusting slowly to the new medication, but it still didn't seem to work in my eyes.

I arrived at New Oaks somewhat apprehensive of what lay ahead, and no sooner had I got through the door than my dad kicked off again. He punched his clenched fist into his other hand in a heated rage. He then started kicking the living crap out of the walls.
'Don't do that David!' said a staff member,
But he still persisted, kicking violently at the wall. I also noticed he had somehow broken his arm!
'MICHAEL, I'M COMING HOME WHETHER YOU LIKE IT OR NOT!' he shouted.
'It's not up to him though Dave!' said the staff member as my dad still tried to kick the wall.

Again I went home feeling upset and depressed. I

wanted my dad back, how he used to be. Schizophrenia was his life now, and how he battled and fought his psychosis would be a struggle to remember. I remember when he had his first breakdown when I was just eight. I was not old enough to understand what was wrong with him. He became very paranoid and left a large note on the kitchen table with the words 'GET OUT YOU!' scribbled in marker pen. He was convinced someone was coming into the flat during the day whilst we were out. 'Everybody has got the same keys on this housing estate' he said.
'People come and go when they please' he said, concerned. It was a very unsettling time for my dad and me, and his memory was not too good either; he would forget about money he had spent and then harshly blame me.

The following week I visited New Oaks again. I arrived and I met up with my dad and it was not long until he kicked off. 'I'M GOING!' he shouted and opened the door to exit the ward. 'DAVID!' the nurses shouted.
My Father was sectioned so he was not allowed out of the ward. He ran and ran whilst the nurses chased him eagerly. 'DAVID COME BACK' shouted the female nurses.
I suddenly caught a glimpse of dad sprinting between the two buildings. His strides were as if he was Linford Christie, never had I seen a man run like that.
'Run like fucking hell' he thought, trying catch his breath.
I stood and watched him and as he ran towards

me, he fell over on the lawn. His hands were covered in blood, like a wounded solider.
'I love you Michael!' he said in a calm voice as the nurses took him back to the ward and cleaned him up.
I was very touched in a way by what had just happened, and again I had to go home, which was a shame as I had not long been there.

A few weeks later they arranged a home visit for my dad. I was apprehensive as I knew how unwell he was and I reluctantly agreed to him coming home for the week. The nurse dropped him off at the house and came in with another patient, a young girl with dark hair. 'The house numbers are funny around here, aren't they?' she said taking a long drag on her cigarette. They left my dad with me, and they told him to behave and they would pick him up on Friday night.

My father had a pillbox with his pills in which the hospital had supplied, all organised ready for him to take over the period of the week. I don't know why but my dad had only been there five minutes and he tried taking all the tablets at once. I tried to stop him but he was still shoving pills in his mouth. He kept barging me out the way, as I desperately tried to call for an ambulance. The operator answered.
'Quick my dad is taking an overdose!' I shouted as he pulled the phone out of the wall.
I plugged the phone back in the wall, and again he tried barging me out the way. The operator phoned back and I gave them the address. It was not long

The Master of the Cube

before the ambulance and police arrived and took him to hospital!

David was in hospital for four years trying to recover from his illness. He tried several different medications and therapies but nothing seemed to work. I did wonder 'will he ever get better?' I thought I just needed to hang in there. As a last resort the doctors tried him on a drug called 'Clozaril' which has helped over 225,000 people with schizophrenia. It was the wonder drug for him. They normally use Clozaril as a last resort and he needed it to get better, which he eventually did.

For the last five years of his life he lived a more normal and settled life. Even though he was in sheltered housing, he got some quality time from his life. We could have conversations like we used to.
'I feel so much better Michael, I can concentrate now' he said, pleased.
'I'm glad the new medication is working for you,' I said
'Yes that Clozaril is working really well, I have to have blood tests every two weeks,' he said.

The Huntington's was more apparent in his life now and he sadly passed away in 2002 at the age of fifty-three. I shall miss him very much…

ULYSSES

DAY 1

21:00 hours. I sat and watched our journey towards Saturn. It seemed to be taking a lifetime, and I found myself squinting my eyes hard to try and negotiate our distance from the beautiful gas giant. We were a mere two days away from the orbit of Saturn, approaching at about 1000kmh, and we were all really tired after being in space for three and half years.

I watched as the turbulent gas storms danced and twisted violently through the dense atmosphere. Saturn was beautiful, graced with its magnificent ring system of giant chunks of ice, all

The Master of the Cube

orbiting at an aggressive rate. Some are really huge and some are like tiny particles of dust. Our first mission objective is to study Saturn's satellites; we also have a planned and difficult procedure to descend through the thick orange haze to land safely on the surface of Titan. The current date is 10th of November 2040. As I leaned back and took a look out of the far window on the left of the cockpit I could clearly see Cassini, an older probe, orbiting the almighty gas globe. Cassini is still relaying data and transmitting valuable pictures back to Earth.

I got up and walked through to the lounge lobby. I walked through several spherical arched doorways until reaching the lobby where 'Jim boy' and 'Michaela' were sat around a small table playing cards and drinking cherry cola.
'Hey Chaz come and join us, what's it looking like out there?' asked Jim boy.
'No real change, everything looks normal!' I reported back to him with a smile,
'Darling, do you want some cola?' asked Michaela in her very strong Russian accent.
'Not just now, I'm feeling a little tired…I think I'll head up' I said with a yawn, wiping my eyes.
'I'll take watch. See you soon Michaela, and you get some rest, Chaz!' said Jim boy, placing his hand on my back, putting his cards down on the table and walking through into the adjacent corridor.
I climbed the ladder to the top of the shaft and squeezed into my cramped quarters and laid down.
'What an astounding and super planet Saturn is, I have never seen anything so beautiful, and we are

finally here' I thought, closing my eyes and listening to relaxation music that my dad had given me.

I always remember my dad would be fast asleep on the floor when I got home from work; why? Well, he would do these relaxation classes at the local hospital as he suffered from anxiety, and he would practice his relaxation at home listening to a cassette tape. He would fall asleep in the process...

'How funny he was' I chuckled to myself with a grin, turning over onto my side and remembering my great father who I had not seen since launch day over three years ago.

23:50 hours. I awoke feeling somewhat achy. So would you if you had been sleeping in cramped quarters for over three years with little room to spare! Let me introduce myself.

My name is 'Chaz Summer' and I work with my two other colleges for NSA, undergoing the deep space programme 'Ulysses' to Saturn. 'Michaela' is of course Russian, she once worked for the U.S.S.R space programme but they collapsed some years ago now. She is a vital part of our mission, and knows everything we actually know about Saturn and its more than sixty satellites. She is very nice, she is fun to be with and has an IQ rating of 145. She is tall with shoulder length blonde hair and her eyes are deep green, the kind of green you see in your average domestic pussy cat. She has been a real support for me as we all have experienced times when we have all got on each other's nerves and I have felt like throttling 'Jim boy', but Michaela luckily has calmed us both down.

Now Jim boy is a little different. 'James' is his real name, although he likes to be called 'Jim boy'. Don't get me wrong, he is a great friend, but he has the tendency to be domineering and tries to be competitive in every aspect of space flight. He is also a great poker player. He has beaten us under the table on several occasions but he can't top me at chess, which frustrates Jim boy greatly to my satisfaction! He is the youngest of the crew. Michaela is the eldest and I'm 32. I have a son called 'Joseph' by the way, he is 9, and I miss him terribly!

00:10 hours: I walked into the cockpit area where Jim boy was sat as we approached 'Rhea', Saturn's second largest moon. Never had I seen so much surface detail of craters and impacts on a body. Jim boy was sat taking notes in the chair.
'Rhea looks interesting, how are you finding it?' I asked Jim boy, sitting down in the opposite chair.
'Well yes, Rhea is much more cratered than I would have thought, but I must admit Titan looks more interesting' said Jim boy, placing his pen behind is ear.
'Yes, I'm really looking forward to checking out Titan' I said.
'Aren't you scared though?' he asked in a soft tone.
'Guess I am, I just hope and pray it does not go wrong and everything goes according to plan' I said hesitantly.
'We have six days till the descent on Titan. Some of

the best engineers in the country worked on Ulysses, and the Lander also has some of the most advanced technology in the world' said Jim boy encouragingly.

'I am just concerned of a sudden technical failure. We are millions of Miles from Earth, who knows what could happen' I said, scratching my chin.

'Yes that is a worry, though the Ulysses Lander is fitted with several fail-safe devices so try not to be too concerned' said Jim boy, admiring Titan again.

'How do you think Michaela feels about the landing?' I asked.

'She's pretty cool about it; she has shit loads of experience, and has been in space several times. She is as hard as nails.' Jim boy said with a smile, taking a sharp gulp from his cola.

'Why don't you ask her yourself? She will be with you all the way' said Jim boy.

'Sure, I'll speak to her tomorrow' I said, watching our slow approach to take our first shots of Rhea.

'What's our current speed?' I asked.

'100kmh. We're almost at Rhea, it won't be much longer now' said Jim boy, moving the flight stick slightly to the right.

After a few short moments we reached Rhea at 00:30 hours. Jim boy set up the cameras to take detailed shots and also to map the entire surface of the satellite.

'There are some real whopping craters here, it certainly has a violent history' I said whilst looking at the photos printing out on the LCD monitors.

'Yes, sure has. It's a little bigger than I expected, don't you agree?' asked Jim boy, changing the cameras angles in succession.

'Yes, it is large I must say. Right, do you need me to set up the sampler dart?' I asked.

'Yes, better get that job done as well, all the technical jargon is over there on the left of the dashboard in that big red book!' he said, still taking shots as I headed over to the dashboard to set up the sampler for examination.

DAY 2

14:02 hours. The sampler dart we jettisoned towards the surface of Rhea discovered the characteristics as an icy body with a density of about 1,233 kg/m^3. This low density indicated that it is made of 25% rocks. The temperature on Rhea is -174°C in direct sunlight and between -200°C and -220°C in the shade. Rhea is heavily cratered and has bright markings on its surface. Some craters are really deep, I must add. Our next analysis is 'Iapetus', Saturn's most unusual moon. One side is as bright as snow, and the other is dark as asphalt which is really bizarre to say the least.

'Michaela, can I ask you something?' I said, calmly leaning against the archway.
'Yes, go ahead, what's wrong?' asked Michaela, a little concerned.
'Do you think the Titan descent will be a success?' I asked, swaying my arms back and forth anxiously.
'Yes I feel confident that Titan will be a success, you must not try to worry. I'll be with you, and Jim boy will be monitoring our progress from Ulysses' she said with a pleasant smile.
'OK, sure, I am just concerned the parachutes won't eject correctly or we will have a bad landing, it's so hard to say with Titan's thick haze' I said, straightening up and sitting down on the couch.
'What makes you feel the mission won't succeed Chaz?' asked Michaela with a slight pause.
'I just have this gut feeling that something's going to go wrong. Maybe I'm worrying too much' I said in a

disgruntled tone.
'You must remember that shuttle disaster of the mid 1980's, that's what I worry about mostly' I said, straightening my cap.
'I see, but remember the shuttle back then had certain safety issues, they have all been eradicated now' said Michaela, crossing her legs.
'If everything goes according to plan, the thing I am mostly looking forward to see is to look up at the sky and then observe Saturn through the clouds' I said with a smile.
'It is the most beautiful object within our solar system, I have been waiting years for this moment Chaz' she said with equal anticipation.
'I'm not totally sure Saturn will be visible through the haze though, but I really hope so,' Michaela said,
'I had better go and help Jim boy. We are approaching iapetus today so I am looking forward to mapping the surface' I said, climbing through the oval arch.

'Hi Jim boy, so we made it to iapetus!' I commented.
'Yes I have started the mapping process. Take a peek at the monitor shots, great, aren't they?' said Jim boy, very excited.
'Yes, it's almost if iapetus was made from two other satellites that collided with each other' I said, studying the moon,
'Yes, light and dark, one ice moon and one dead moon I guess' said Jim boy, changing the camera angles once more.
'I wonder if the dark side has a different

composition from the light?' I asked Jim boy.

'Highly likely. It's made from different materials. I will ask Michaela' replied Jim boy.

'I'll set up the sampler dart!' I said, preparing to jettison the dart deep into the surface.

I was starting to become increasingly anxious about the Titan descent.

'Why am I so worried about the parachutes?' I asked myself like a paranoid android.

'I must not worry. Michaela will know the score' I thought to myself whilst setting up the second dart for analysis.

DAY 3

16:00 hours. Michaela sat and watched the beauty of Saturn as we were now in complete orbit of the giant planet. Michaela studied the turbulent ring system and took a closer look at the weather patterns, slightly tilting her head to one side.
'Saturn is sure violent; it looks so calm and peaceful from Earth' thought Michaela, somewhat perplexed.

The wind speeds we had calculated were as high as 1000mph, with flashing harsh lightning bolts deep within Saturn's dense clouds creating patterns near the equator. Michaela sat and pondered, pinching her arm every so often to see she was not dreaming. She had spent her whole life studying Saturn and now she felt somewhat dismissive that she was really there. It reminded her of when 'Buzz Aldrin' set foot on the moon in 1969 and he then started to act strangely when he came back to Earth after seeing the Earth so small.

'Michaela is acting odd' I thought as I watched her intensely.
'Michaela, are you alright?' I asked, concerned.
'Yes, I am fine, it's just simply beautiful Chaz' she said.
'I'm actually quite taken aback by the magnificent ring system. I have never seen so many chunks of ice!' she remarked again, looking somewhat vague.
'Was she going crazy?' I then asked myself.

'She is talking sense, but she was acting really weird' I thought a little bemused.
'Have you been sleeping alright?' I asked her.
'Nope, not really, I have not been able to sleep for the last two days, it's all the excitement I guess' said Michaela.
'Don't you think you ought to try and get some rest?' I asked her.
'Don't forget we have a very important descent in two days, so please don't let us down' I said in a forceful tone.
'I'll try', she said, climbing up into the quarters area.

'Jim boy, I am a little worried about Michaela, she is acting a little strange' I said sitting down.
'Oh really, she's just tired, she will be fine' said Jim boy, taking more storms analyses.
'Yes I guess so…she seems a bit vague, don't you think? I asked him.
'I can't say I have really noticed,' remarked Jim boy scratching his nose.
'Maybe I am reading too much into it, I have become an anxious wreck these days' I chuckled.
'Yeah, just chill man', said Jim boy with a frown…

DAY 4

12:34 hours. The day before the Titan land, and there have been some really catastrophic complications. Michaela is just not well enough to take part in the landing. We are both now really concerned for her, but we have a clear mission orders from NSA to proceed as planned. We will have intermittent transmissions with Earth during our descent. We don't know what we will touch down on, petrol, sea, snow or rocks. Without Michaela's guidance and knowledge we will have to rely heavily on Huston ground control centre.

'What a real shame for Michaela, do you think she will ever return to reality?' I asked, looking at Jim boy preparing for the landing.
'I really hope so, I thought you were just paranoid about her behavior' said Jim boy.
'You know it's really scary, it reminds me of my father when he had his breakdown' he said.
'Your father had a breakdown!' I remarked surprised.
'Yeah, you can be the coolest dude in the world and still develop mental health issues,' he said whilst checking the electrics of the Ulysses Lander.
'So what happened exactly?' I asked with an inquisitive posture.
'Well, he just got really depressed after my mother left him, and it was all down hill from there on. He became like a child, and he also became very paranoid' said Jim boy.
'Paranoid…about what?' I asked.

'He just thought people were always talking about him, plots and weird stuff like that,' he said, double checking the electrics.

'That must have been hard on your dad,' I said, pouring some cola into a cup.
'Yeah it was, and on me!' remarked Jim boy with an almighty frown.
'I wouldn't wish it on anyone, that's for sure,' he said.
'I remember I got really paranoid after smoking too much weed once!' I giggled.
'Yeah, that stuff is really mental, like when you get the munchies, the number of 'Corn dogs' I got through is amazing really', said Jim, lightening up.
'You dad used to play the guitar, didn't he?' I asked.
'He was not that great though, I think he would have been better off playing the Triangle!' laughed Jim boy.
'Why the hell did they make us play those crap musical instruments at school? I mean the Triangle, I ask myself!' I said sarcastically.
'Yeah school, I remember when we had a real thing about William Tufnell's lunch box', he said.
'Oh,' I said.
'We would wind him right up…We often pinched his lunch box, and then ran around the playground with it!' said Jim.
'The funny thing was he used to get so wound up, he would go bright red in the cheeks, and he would chase us whilst sticking out his tongue. He looked like a red tomato with a spasmodic worm poking out!' said Jim, laughing hysterically.
'He he' I laughed as we tried to be serious.

The Master of the Cube

'Right all joking aside… The drop is tomorrow, let's get some rest, son' said Jim.

DAY 5

The Descent

14:00 hours, the afternoon of the launch. All was going well so far although I awoke nervous about our complicated landing. There is still no change in Michaela's condition. She is still too unwell and not fit for work, which is a real blow for my anxiety state.
'I guess her seeing Saturn up so close just blew her mind.' I felt upset. 'Like Buzz,' I thought. 'Yes, Buzz' I thought again.
'We will just have to look after her now, she needs us and our support…God…I hope nothing goes wrong' I muttered to myself with an eerie feeling in my gut.

We were both suited and booted, zipped up ready, helmets tightly fixed on our hi-tech Cosmo naught suits as we stepped into the small cramped Ulysses Lander.
The Ulysses Lander is a little bit like the Apollo Lander of the sixties but of course with much more hi-tech architecture and a robust shell to withstand what ever Titan will throw at us.

We both sat in our pilot seats, strapped ourselves securely in place, and then started the ignition sequence and countdown,
'Huston we are ready for launch, all systems are go' I said, speaking anxiously into my helmet com port.

The Master of the Cube

'Ulysses receiving you loud and clear,' replied Huston.
Huston, begin the countdown' I said.
'Commencing countdown...10...9...8...7...6...5...4...3...2...1...0, chocks away!' I shouted as the clamps released the big bird into the sky.

'Huston...we are on our way, launch was successful' said Jim boy as we headed towards Titan's dense and cloudy atmosphere fading into the orange soup.
We entered Titan's clouds quickly at first, and then we began to slow as the Ulysses parachutes engaged, bringing Ulysses to a gradual descent. The haze was really thick. We slowly penetrated the fog; Methane rain began falling downward toward the petrol oceans below. I could clearly make out distinct shore lines and waves.
'Wow, look at that!' I said with delight.
We could now clearly see Saturn visible through the clouds over the horizon; the atmosphere was becoming less thick as our altitude began to drop.
'Its beautiful, just bloody beautiful!' shouted Jim boy, lighting up like a small child opening his Xmas presents.

The sky was just 'fucking mind blowing!' Beautiful colours with shimmering oily oceans that sparkled as Saturn looked down from the heavens above.
We became ever closer. More and more surface detail became apparent; mountain ranges covered in snow and ice crevasses and rivers running through, even giant waterfalls, or petrol falls I

should say.
'Look at those falls' I said.
'Yeah there real cool' said Jim boy.
'All systems are normal. We will just have to be patient and we'll hit the surface within 30 minutes' said Jim boy.

15:20 hours. The slow descent was a very beautiful exhilarating experience and so far everything had gone according to plan. We reached the surface at 15:49 hours and it was not a bumpy ride at all.
'Thank God!' I thought quietly to myself as the anxiety lifted for the meantime.
'You ready bud?' asked Jim boy as we turned the valve and then unlocked the airlock door, stepping out onto the surface of Titan.
I went first and then Jim boy slowly followed.
'The first man ever to step foot on another world other than the moon,' I thought to myself, with a proud posture.
The surface of Titan was strange. Large snow balls littered the baron landscape for miles, and also I could see drifting snow was all around us. It was still raining, Methane rain, the rain drops were large and fell in a really bizarre way.
'What the hell caused these large snow balls to form do you think?' I asked, puzzled.
'I don't know...they're a really unusual size too' said Jim Boy wiping his helmet visor clean.
'Let's put the flag up!' I said in an excited tone.
'Sure, let's christen Titan' said Jim boy, thrusting the American flag deep into the snow.
We walked around for a bit, gazed up at the sky and wondered how an earth we had made it.

The Master of the Cube

'We have done it…' I thought, relieved.

'Hey let's make the first cosmic snowman!' said Jim Boy.
'What…?' I replied.
'You know, the first snowman to be built in outer space' said Jim boy, gathering up the deep snow and ice.
'Got ya, nice idea' I said with a little chuckle.
'Hey, it reminds me of when I was kid, building snow men and all that' I said, gathering up the snow into a giant fuck off boulder.
'Yeah it sure does, Chaz' said Jim boy.
'Pass me those two small rocks. We can use them as his eyes' I said, placing the smaller boulder on top of the large one for his head.
'Blimey, he's the biggest dude in the universe!' laughed Jim boy, as we both enjoyed our childish moment…

Some time later...

'Let's head over to those canyons over there, I am just curious to see what is up there' said Jim.
'Sure…but we must be careful!' I remarked as walked towards the canyons.
We walked for a few moments when suddenly Jim slipped!
He slid down a small ice crevasse holding his leg in agony.

'Fuck, my leg!' said Jim screwing his eyes up, as his visor misted up,
'Hold right there, I'm coming to get you' I said in a

hurried tone.
'No it's too dangerous, shit my oxygen tanks are leaking!' shouted Jim boy as oxygen profusely projected from his tanks.
'You must have ruptured them in the fall!' I said in a panic stricken voice.

'No, I'm coming to get you, here take my hand' I said.
'No Chaz, I can't reach, it's too late, you only have a short supply of oxygen, leave me here' said Jim boy, becoming weaker, losing oxygen at a rapid rate.
'I can't breathe...I just can't...' said Jim boy and he suddenly started to undo his visor.
"What in Fuck are you doing?' I shouted.
'It's no good Chaz...leave me here...' he said as he opened his visor and his face became an unbearable sight to look at.
'No...No...' I said as I wept like a child.
'What in the fuck had gone wrong?' I asked, 'He is dead, my best pal is dead...I knew this would happen' I thought as I scampered back to Ulysses lender in floods of tears.

He had taken his own life to save another...

What a brave man...I just could not get the vision out of my head of Jim boy opening his visor and his face turning to a horrid mess...It was a real shame...

As the days passed I did make it back to the Ulysses, and...Yes, Michaela did recover

eventually. I was just saddened that she could not see the delights of Titan for the first time.
Titan was a beautiful place, full of magic and to see Titan was a true enlightenment and it gave me a much better understanding of our solar system and how the universe works.
Who knows where we will head to in the future, Jupiter maybe? Neptune? Or even beyond our own solar system and into interstellar space...

Maybe we will find intelligent life? Live on and populate another world or moon, rule the galaxy, what do you think?

MASTER OF THE CUBE

Andrew sat in his English class. He was your average fourteen-year-old boffin, but he was no ordinary teenager; he was clever and unique. Andrew looked the part with his uncomfortable 80's hairdo, thick rimmed specs and crooked tie. He was good at everything, English, Maths, Chemistry, you name it, he was good at it. People called him 'square eyes' but Andrew just ignored their ignorance and studied hard. He wanted to be a scientist when he left school.

Andrew was heavily into computers. He had a 'ZX81' which he programmed in machine code and he was eagerly awaiting for the 'ZX82', known nowadays as the 'ZX spectrum'. The Spectrum boasted of colour, real keys and sound. His main passion was programming games of course, so he was really looking forward to the Spectrum release. The Spectrum had hi-res graphics, better than the block monochrome graphics of its predecessors.

Andrew also claimed he could solve the 'Rubik Cube' in about 25 seconds!
He was like the young 'Einstein' mathematical Genius as he worked out his equations in his textbook.

'Andrew Wills! Pay attention, put the pen down and listen!' shouted Mr Jones.
'Sorry Sir' Andrew said quietly and closed his textbook.

The Master of the Cube

Andrew's mind would drift off. He would wonder if there was life on other planets and if time travel could really be possible.

Meanwhile...

'Andrew's very smart, but he lives in a dream world!' said his dad, straightening his tie for work.
'All he does is hang around with that Phoebe Blight girl!' said Andrew's dad.
'Yes, but they are very close Ben' said Celia.
'Why does he not get some male friends? I don't think its healthy for him, he needs to mix with boys his own age' said Ben.
'Phoebe is a nice girl, don't take that away from Andrew'! snapped Celia.
'OK, I'm off to work' said Ben, kissing his wife goodbye on the cheek.

Celia was really mellow, a caring and an understanding mother. She had long blonde hair, and hazel eyes, which reflected kindness and love. Andrew's father was stern, strict and had worked for 'IBM' for several years. Celia loved to read, she loved reading the latest women's magazines, and she also had a passion to write poetry. Celia was also a spiritual lady; she often read the Tarot and believed in spirit energies. She had a belief because often her deceased grandmother would visit her and sit on the end of her bed when she was little.

Andrew liked Phoebe. 'Mad old Phoebe' they would call her. She was into white magic and loved Punk and Metal. Her hair was black with purple streaks; her eyes were as dark as sapphires. Andrew's father disapproved of Phoebe as he thought she was a bit weird and could be a bad influence on his son.

Andrew met up with Phoebe at break time and they both sat in the sun on the lawns of the school. 'Petersburg secondary school' was a good school, had a good reputation, lovely gardens and a large playing field. The weather had been really nice over the last few weeks in hot July and the playing field was littered with pupils. Screams of joy and laughter could be heard all around the school as everyone was enjoying the midday sun.

'Did you finish your science project, Andy?' asked Phoebe.
'Yes, it was easy, too easy' said Andrew, straightening his specs.
'I'm looking forward to a new science project next week, on the cosmos' said Andrew, flicking back his hair.
'That science teacher...I hate Mr Henderson! He's a right nut!' said Phoebe.
'Take no notice of his aggression, he shouldn't be teaching here anyway!' said Andrew sternly.
'Why shouldn't he be teaching here?' asked Phoebe curiously,
'Apparently he hit a pupil!' he said, again straightening his specs.
'Oh, golly' said Phoebe with a look of disgust, and tucked into her peanut butter sandwich.

The Master of the Cube

Andrew like Phoebe, he liked her a lot, but he knew she would never see past his thick rimmed glasses.
'She won't want me' thought Andrew, feeling some what guilty.
Phoebe was still sitting and eating her sandwich when she became very excited.

'Look, it's him, that really nice one!' said Phoebe with a dreamy look in her eyes.

Yes, it was jake, 'the scruffy looser', Andrew thought.

He was the king of scruff. He wore 'Dr Marten' boots with about a thousand eyelets, and a long black jacket. He had long swaying black hair and in Andrew's eyes he was a creep!
'Why him?' he thought.
'I know he likes metal, but he is the Antichrist or at least he could be!' Andrew thought.
'Perhaps he's possessed!' thought Andrew as Phoebe continued to look at Jake walking across the playground.
'Why did his parents let him dress so badly? And his scruffy uniform looks like it has seen better days,' thought Andrew,

'He's too old for you Phoebe' said Andrew, concerned.
'What, are you jealous or something?' said Phoebe very defensively.
'No of course not, he's just a bit weird that's all, I just don't trust him,' said Andrew with a look of disbelief.

'What?' said Phoebe.
'I'm just looking out for you Phoebe,' he said, again straightening his specs.
'I'm old enough to look after myself thank you very much!' snapped Phoebe as she packed up her things and stormed off in a sulk.
'Phoebe, I'm sorry!' shouted out Andrew, but Phoebe kept on walking,
'How could she fancy such a creep?' he thought as the bell went for the end of break time.

Later that evening...

'Hi Phoebe, I'm really sorry about earlier,' said Andrew in an apologetic tone.
'That's OK Andy, I'm sorry for storming off' said Phoebe.
'Want to come round?' she asked.
'Yeah sure, what time? I have a new game I have done and I would really like you see it,' said Andrew
'What's your new game called?' asked Phoebe with a slight pause.
'Swilly Willy!' said Andrew, somewhat embarrassed.
'What?' said Phoebe in fits of giggles.
'You nut,' she laughed.
'Anyway I look forward to seeing it,' said Phoebe,
'See you in about 20 minutes, is that OK?' asked Phoebe with a giggle.
'Yeah sure,' said Andrew.
'OK Andy,' said Phoebe as she put down the receiver.

Phoebe was looking forward to seeing Andy as she had a great idea to discuss with him; she wanted

The Master of the Cube

Andy to enter the Rubik cube championships in school.
'Will he do it? He's highly capable but will his dad approve?' Phoebe sat and asked herself.
Phoebe hated Ben, she could not stand Andy's dad but really appreciated his mother's kindness and charm.
'There goes the front door bell!' thought Phoebe and rushed downstairs to open the front door.
To her astonishment Jake was stood there looking weird as per usual.

'Hi, you Phoebe?' asked Jake.
'Yes...what do you want?' she asked, puzzled.
'I hear you play Bass! I am starting a metal band, fancy joining?' he asked with a smile.
'Metal band...oh...well, yes', she said obliged.
'See ya at the school hall tomorrow after school', he said walking away into the sun.
'Se ya', called out Phoebe, but he did not turn around, he just kept on walking as Phoebe's heart began to pound ten to the dozen!
Phoebe stood weak in the knees.
'God, he's the man,' thought Phoebe, despite his weirdness.

Phoebe loved boys with long hair; she loved Jake's silky black hair especially.
His jacket was covered in interesting patterns and his piercing blue eyes would almost hypnotize Phoebe, leaving her in a vulnerable state. Shortly thereafter Andrew arrived...

'Hi Mrs Blight', Andrew shouted through to the

kitchen.

'Oh hi Andrew, was school fine today?' asked Phoebe's mother.

'Yes, fine Mrs Blight,' Andrew replied, straightening his specs.

'Here, let me take your jacket Andy,' said Phoebe.

'Hold on, just let me get my cassette tape out of my pocket', said Andrew, pulling the tape out of his top jacket pocket.

'Hey, is that the game you were telling me about on the phone?' Phoebe asked, taking his coat and hanging it on the banister.

'Yes' replied Andrew, placing the tape in his shirt pocket.

'I hope it loads OK, sometimes it doesn't!' said Andrew with a smile.

They both rushed upstairs into Phoebe's dad's computer room...

Andrew's computer game was mad, really mad; he had several levels to the game so far and it was kind of based along the lines of snakes and ladders. He named his sprite 'Swilly Willy' after having a hilarious discussion with his older brother rolling about the floor in fits of laughter. Andrew's brother Darren was sound, he loved motorbikes and he worked in a chocolate factory five days a week. He was large of course, ate way too much and was funny as you like! Darren was nothing like his younger brother in the respect that he was not as clever as Andrew, but he was a very good listener...

Phoebe and Andy sat together, switched on the computer and placed the tape in the cassette

The Master of the Cube

recorder.

'Right, here we go, let's see,' said Andrew straightening his specs for a further time.

'You always straighten your glasses, don't you?' said Phoebe with a grin,

'Yes, it's just a habit, I have always done it,' said Andrew, watching the screen.

'Swilly Willy...where did you get that crazy name from?' asked Phoebe.

'Oh, my brother thought of it, he's a bit mad you know,' said Andy with a little chuckle.

'Right, you need to climb the ladders and collect all the strawberries to reach the top before you are captured by the toilet king!' he said.

'The toilet king... ha! You fruit loop and your brother!' said Phoebe in fits of laughter.

'Looks good Andy, pretty darn wacky too!' said Phoebe.

Phoebe did not dare to tell Andrew about Jake. She knew what would happen if she told him, as she knew he clearly disapproved of Jake. All the time Phoebe sat and played the game all she could think about was Jake, how he had asked her to play bass with him. Phoebe loved the bass guitar, she had a 'Fender' bass that she polished everyday. The bass was white with a black linear 'Marilyn Monroe' mural on the scratch plate. She was a good bassist, self taught, and Jake had heard through the school music group that she was the bee's knees. Jake played the guitar; he played it well although the darker side of music was his genre, rather along the lines of 'Sabbath' and 'Judas Priest'.

'Do you like it, Phoebe?' asked Andrew.

'Hello...Phoebe?' he asked, but Phoebe seemed not be listening.

'Hello... Earth calling Bongo?' asked Andrew.

'I beg your pardon...', said Phoebe.

'Do you like the game...?' asked Andrew, a little frustrated.

'Yes...It's great, really funny, ' said Phoebe a little vaguely.

'Something on your mind...want to talk?' asked Andy concerned.

'Oh, it's nothing really, but there is something I would like to discuss with you Andy,' she said, lightly placing her hand on his knee.

Andrew became a little excited,

'Is she going to pop the question? Surely not,' thought Andrew with feelings of guilt churning up his insides.

'Have you seen the school notice in the hall?' she asked.

'Darn bang goes another dream!' thought Andrew, trying to hide his disheartened feelings,

'No I haven't,' he said.

'Well they are having a senior Rubik cube championship in school in two weeks time, are you interested?' asked Phoebe, hoping he would say yes.

'I guess so...', he said, again straightening his specs.

The following evening...

Phoebe had spent a lot of time in front of the mirror, getting ready for Jake. Andy still did not know about

The Master of the Cube

it. She was worried he would find out sooner or later. Phoebe packed her bass into her gig case with her leads and packed up her practice amp. Her dad was going to give her a lift to the school hall to have her first rehearsal with 'Black magic', the local school band.

They pulled up outside the school. Phoebe kissed her dad goodbye and headed across the grass carrying her 'bit of plank' as her dad would always call it. She entered the hall; they were all there apart from Jake. Odd balls they all were to say the least. One in particular was the oddest, and he had a Mohican with bursts of colour in his crown and a big bolt in his nose. 'Golly...what a bunch of weirdos,' thought Phoebe, but it was fine, she liked weird people.

'Hi...you must be Phoebe no doubt? Jack's the name', said the one with the painful looking bolt through his nose.
'Yes, I'm here for rehearsals', said Phoebe, quietly looking at his electrifying hair.
Suddenly the doors to the hall flew open and in walked Jake.

'How's it hanging dudes?' he shouted.
'Jake me old mate!' shouted the greasy one with the leathers.
'Hi spud nose!' Jake said, hugging the one with the deranged bolt through his nostrils.
'Phoebe, glad you could make it... Ready for some jazz?' he asked.
'Er...yes...sure...sounds cool,' she said a little

nervously.

'God, if Andy were here he would go mad!' thought Phoebe.

'But what he doesn't know can't hurt him I suppose...' she thought guiltily.

'Better get tuned up guys', said the greasy one whilst picking his nose.

A few minutes later and after a lot of noise everyone was tuned up and ready for action.

'The song is called 'Devil's daughter', got it? It is in F by the way', said Jake to Phoebe.

'Sure Jake', she said, flustered.

The drummer started banging the living crap out of the drums. 'Talk about psycho! Bloody hell,' thought Phoebe in utter astonishment. He was the drummer from hell.

'Any more of this and he will give me a bloody headache!' thought Phoebe, covering her ears.

'The noise is terrible; a load of noisy bollocks,' she thought, dissatisfied.

'Jake's a good guitarist though,' she thought keenly. She admired his 'Les Paul' guitar with decals of skulls. He was playing it like a rampant steam wagon.

'THE DEVIL SAT IN HELL!' shouted out the lead singer.

'Oh my gosh who's that nutcase?', she thought.

'What a load of crap! God, they're terrible,' she thought, trying to follow the music.

'Help... Get me out of this nut hole...' she thought,

The Master of the Cube

and she could not wait till it was all over.
Phoebe found herself constantly looking at her watch to see when it was 9 o'clock.

Eventually the time came to pack up.
'Enjoy that Phoebe?', asked TJake.
'Er...well...yes...great', said Phoebe, lying out of her back teeth.
'What a horrid experience, never again,' thought Phoebe.
'I don't know how I'm going tell Jake though,' she thought, very concerned,
'Shall I walk you home?', asked Jake.
'Yes I would like that,' she said.

Phoebe had noticed that TJake had his eye on her all night. She was sure she was in for a treat, but not all went according to plan...
Little did she know that Jake was not all he seemed. He was devious, and sexually untrustworthy. He had already been cautioned for minor sex offences for exposing himself to young women, in other words he was a pig!

Dusk had fallen on the town; the street lamps cast colourful orange glints on the roads, lighting up the street like a racetrack. The night was peaceful. She could hear the echoes of the teenagers playing football in the park, and the birds chirping their night song in the trees, which sounded delightful. They both walked slowly, humping their guitars around as they walked into the setting sun.

'Hey, I know a short cut, through the alley,' said

Jake, kissing Phoebe on the lips.
They both stopped and Phoebe wrapped her arms around him and kissed him passionately.
'Come on Phoebe, let's get moving into that alley,' said Jake, pulling her arm towards the dark alley.
Phoebe began to become a tad worried as she was only fifteen and did not therefore want to go too quickly.
'Come on, what are you waiting for?' asked Jake, still pulling her towards the alley.
'No, I don't want to... Please!' she said reluctantly.
'I know you want to Phoebe', he said,
'NO JAKE NO!' she yelled.
'Keep your voice down, you silly cow!' said TJake quietly but aggressively.
The realisation had hit her, was he going to rape her? Or worst still kill her?
How on earth could she get it so wrong? she thought as she struggled to get away.
'GET YOUR HANDS OF ME, MUM!' she screamed.
Suddenly there was someone standing on the other side of the street.
'GET YOUR DIRTY HANDS OFF HER YOU FREAK!' a voice shouted.
'Who's that?' thought Phoebe.
'Sounds like Andy, can't be...' she thought as she kicked Jake in the nuts!
Jake fell to the floor holding his crutch and Phoebe run like hell towards Andy.
'Come on, let's get out of here before psycho gets back up!' said Andrew in a hurried tone.
'YOU'RE WELCOME TO HER, FOUR EYES!' shouted Jake across at them as they ran in through Andrew's front door.

The Master of the Cube

'How did you know it was me?' she asked Andrew, still shaken.

'I heard your screams. It happened right outside my front door which was lucky,' said Andrew, hugging Phoebe.

'I told you he couldn't be trusted, didn't I?' said Andrew.

'Why did you lie to me Phoebe, what the hell were you doing?' said Andrew.

No answer...

'Well...?' he asked, waiting for an answer.

'Because I knew you would be like this...' said Phoebe, starting to cry.

'Why were you with him?' he asked.

'He came round and wanted me to join his poxy band,' said Phoebe.

'Come on, I'll make you a cup of tea...' he said as they walked into the kitchen.

Andrew sat with Phoebe; he held her hand and comforted her as she began again to sob with disappointment.

'How could I get it so wrong?' she sobbed.

'You just can't trust anyone these days, no one will hurt you as much as people do,' said Andrew compassionately.

'He's a pig, all he wanted me for was sex,' she said in a troubled tone.

'Some guys are like that unfortunately,' said Andrew.

'You deserve better,' he said.

'You're so kind Andy,' she said, kissing him on the cheek.

'She kissed me, surely not me?' Andrew asked

himself.

'I'll look after you Phoebe, I'll protect you from scum like him,' he said, holding her hand tightly.

'Phoebe...can I tell you something...?' asked Andy.

'Yes...what is it?' replied Phoebe.

'Well...I adore you...I love you,' said Andrew, looking down at the floor.

Phoebe clasped Andrew's chin and pushed it upwards so she could see his blushing face.

'Don't worry, you don't need to be embarrassed,' she said with a warm smile.

'I adore you too...but not in that way,' said Phoebe calmly.

'Oh...sorry...OK, I'm just a little disappointed that's all,' he said with a tear in his eye.

'I'm sure you will meet someone who will feel the same...what about my sister?'

'What, Kaleigh?' asked Andrew, surprised.

'How do you feel about her?' she asked.

'Isn't she a little young for me?' he asked.

'No, she's only just turned fourteen, I would go for it. She likes you, I know that much,' said Phoebe, smiling.

'Likes me how...?' he said.

'She told me so. Talk to her tomorrow, she would really like that, but she is very shy,' she said, clasping his chin.

'I can't, I won't know what to say, I always blush and say the wrong thing,' said Andrew.

'No, you'll be fine, just be yourself, anyway she thinks you're intelligent,' she said with a smile.

'I'll help you talk to her, don't worry,' she said as the kettle came to the boil...

The Master of the Cube

One week later; the day of the cube...

Several school boffins had entered the championships, looking the part with their specs. Andrew sat and waited for his name to be called to challenge for the school cup. The next pupil to take the stand was Dominic. He stood as they jumbled up the Rubik cube for him to take the challenge. A large digital timer was above him to time his attempt. He was zany and was regarded as being a smart arse.

'Get ready!' said Mr Henderson.
'Go!' shouted the teacher.
The pupils became excited; they all started shouting out at him like they were at a football match.
He rapidly fiddled with the cube, changing the cube's position as the counter reached 20 seconds!
'Come on, smart arse!' someone shouted.
'You can do it, smarty-pants!' shouted another.
26, bang! Dominic slammed the solved cube down on the table, as the clock stopped.
'Twenty six!' shouted Mr Henderson.
'Wow!' he said.
'Last contestant please, Andrew Wills?' asked Mr Henderson.
Phoebe eagerly watched Andy as he took the stage and she egged him on.
'Go on square eyes! You can do it!' shouted the audience.
'Ready...' said the science teacher.
'GO!' he shouted.
Andrew's mathematical mind went into overdrive,

fixed on the complexity of the cube.
Andrew turned, swivelled the matching colours as the timer reached 20 seconds.
The sweat began to perspire on his brow, as he knew he had only seconds.
'Come on Andy!' shouted out Phoebe.
He had to do it, do it for Phoebe, 23 seconds, Bang!
Andrew slammed the solved cube down on the table.
'God, you've done it!' said Mr Henderson in amazement.
'THE NEW MASTER OF THE CUBE!' shouted the science teacher, as Andrew smiled and lapped up the pupil's cheers. He then looked at Phoebe, straightening his specs one more time.

The following day...

Phoebe smiled back and thought 'Andrew you're the bee's knees!'
'You did it, I knew you could do it,' she said as they both sat eating their packed lunches.
'You're the greatest!' said Phoebe, tucking into her peanut butter sandwich.

Andrew had grown to accept that Phoebe did not love him the way he wanted her to. He had built a strong relationship with Kaleigh. They were very much in love and Andrew graduated as MSC in 1988 at Cambridge University...

Andrew wanted to follow in his idol's footsteps, the wonderful mind of Stephen Hawking. He studied

The Master of the Cube

hard for four years in cosmology and he was a class pupil...
He is still with Kaleigh to this day... Get up there, square eyes!

The tragic Hollywood love affair

Hollywood, America 1950, a sunny beautiful day and one want-to-be-star Scarlet Lanbrook woke on the glorious Saturday in late July. Scarlet sat up, looked across at her handsome boyfriend David and sparked up her first cigarette of the day. She took a deep long drag on her Marlboro, and sat excited about her audition for the film.

Scarlet was really beautiful, all the men thought so, and they would literally fall over themselves to have a chance of being with her. Scarlet had white blonde hair styled by one of the finest 40's stylists 'Shina', her hair shone and reflected delight in the hot sun upon the men's hungry eyes. Her eyes were a deep pastel green, she was the most beautiful girl I had ever set eyes on, and I fell in love with her at a first glance when I met her in 1950.

My name is Markus Johansson. I am a scriptwriter for the Hollywood film industry. I write romantic scripts, as I am a sensitive and romantic kind of guy. There is not any doubt that Scarlet broke my heart; here's my story of Scarlet and I...

Hollywood studios, October 1950. The first day I set my eyes on her, I was standing alongside one of the cameramen, 'Sid' as we called him. He was loud, loved baseball and he would chase his dream of becoming a 'Rock 'n' Roll' star.
He was a bit of a 'Teddy boy', he was a sleek looking fucker too, with big bulging pale blue eyes. He played the guitar in his band 'The Conventionals', a Rock 'n' Roll band originally from Pittsburgh that he had a moderate following from, but Sid wanted the big time.
He was noisy - always! He would dance around the studio holding a hairbrush in his right hand and he sang loudly into it, trying to win the girls. The girls would giggle, egging him on until his head would bulge with his massive ego. I always thought his was a bit of a prick really!

It was fair to say I was a little shy of girls, not as outgoing as Sid, but Scarlet wanted me, not him. Scarlet was looking for a sensitive man, she hated these big headed arrogant types, so Sid was not really ever on her radar. I stood with a cigarette in my mouth, with my blond hair and my black casual suit, then I looked up and there she was...
She was tying her shoelace at the time, unaware that I was looking at her. She finished with her shoes and then she looked up at me. She paused...The look on her face was apparent, she looked ever so thrown back and I could tell by her body language that she was in love.

I noticed she was trying to hide her feelings from me, she would pretend that nothing was wrong, but I knew she had just set eyes on her prince.

I felt woozy, I was totally bowled over by this beautiful woman. She was pretty and dressed really nicely. Her voice was soft, sophisticated with a friendly and polite tone, and she was very much liked amongst the crew. At first I did not have much chance to mix with her; I only write the script, I am not the director and she was the beautiful star. Sid would try and impress her with his egotistical singing and she would laugh at him, but with an awkward posture. She wanted me, not him, as she looked across at me with a dreamy look in her eyes.

We are starting filming on a film named 'Fields of Barley' starring Derek Simpleton, Jason Lampard and Scarlet Lanbrook. This was Scarlet's first film after passing her audition; she had all the right factors, and of course lots of acting talent. The story is about a love triangle between the three actors, which ends in tragedy. I wanted to oversee the making of my new story and this was my fourth consecutive film after the others were a great success.

'Ok, Scarlet, stand over there with Derek, we need to make this look right sweetheart' said Jonathan the director.
'Sure thing' said Scarlet, glancing at Derek.

The first scene was to be shot in the middle of a

cornfield at sunset, a very romantic setting with beautiful pinks and reds descending the skyline. There was a light breeze that particular evening. Birds and crickets could be heard amongst the surroundings and Scarlet just looked beautiful.

'Hold Scarlet in your arms Derek, OK...Action!' said the director in his chair.

'Oh Jake, don't leave me alone here for too long, I will miss you terribly' said Scarlet looking into Derek's eyes with a single tear.
'CUT! Put some more passion into it Scarlet!' said Jonathan in a forceful tone.

'Remember your supposed to be in love...OK...Action!' he said.

'Oh Jake, don't leave me alone here for too long, I will miss you terribly' said Scarlet looking into Derek's eyes with a single tear.
'I'm sorry I have to go for a while...I will be back Sherilyn, back soon,' said Derek, hugging her tightly.
'When I get back we will be together always, I promise you Sherilyn,' he said as they both exchanged a kiss.

'Lucky git!' I suddenly thought.

'Cut!' the director said.
'That's much better Scarlet, more stuff like that baby!' he said,

As the evening drew to a close Scarlet slowly approached me.

'Hi...I'm Scarlet, who are you sweetheart?' she asked calmly.
'Oh hi, my name is Markus...I'm the scriptwriter. I guess you enjoying the acting?' I asked her with my brow slightly raised.
'Yes...I love your hair' she remarked looking at my fringe.
'Thank you' I replied.
'See you around tomorrow' she said, turning around and smiling.
'Yes...see you' I said, admiring her long legs.

Later that evening at my home...

I sat on the bed with my girlfriend at the time, Cynthia, and I reflected on the first day of filming.

'Scarlet...Oh Scarlet' I thought guiltily because I was thinking of a woman other than Cynthia.
I felt like a teenager all over again. I had seen the girl of my dreams. There was a picture of Scarlet on the wall promoting the upcoming film. I looked at it intensely, then my girlfriend undressed.
'Come on Markus...let's make love' she said, shoving her chest in my face.
I guiltily began to undress, undoing my tie frantically as Cynthia began to breathe heavily.
She threw me on the water bed, and sat on top of me, running her nails up and down my stomach and chest, as I became aroused looking at Scarlet's picture.

The Master of the Cube

I felt so guilty as Cynthia pounded up and down on my groin as I watched Scarlet's picture, seeing her face all the time which made me feel dirty and ashamed.

I turned over after making love as Cynthia kissed me goodnight on the cheek...

I lay there for several hours feeling guilty.
'I hope Cynthia doesn't find out...' I thought.
I had betrayed Cynthia in my mind, which hurt me somewhat.

The next day at the studio...

Scarlet came to the set. She looked beautiful and a little nervous. Maybe she was nervous because she had a big day ahead of her, or she was nervous because of me.
She quickly glanced at me then looked away and glanced back at me again. My heart began to pound with excitement. She walked towards me and smiled and brushed herself gently up against me, although she did not speak.

I smelt her perfume as she passed which I could almost taste in my mouth. I felt my body heave slightly with adrenaline. I was seriously head over heels, but I still did not really know her but it felt like she was the one.
'She has to be' I thought quietly, looking back at her.
She again walked towards me and this time she whispered something in my ear.

'Meet me after the set, I want to tell you something' she whispered erotically.
She spoke softly which almost hypnotized me. It made me feel woozy and relaxed.
'Tell me what?' I thought, intrigued.
This left me nervous for the rest of the day; my nerves just kept jangling as I hoped what she would say would be mutual.
'Cynthia would kill me!' I thought ashamed.
'I'm not sort of guy to have an affair,' I thought.

Later that evening...

I met scarlet after the shoot as we both walked out onto the streets of Hollywood. We walked slowly as she told me about her life and her dreams. We both sparked up a cigarette together and suddenly it started to spit with rain. We put up our large umbrella and we walked arm in arm towards the town. The town was busy, the lights had come on and the roads were dampening with the rain, which reflected the colourful town lights, which looked awesome in late October.
We both stopped outside 'Mandy's Cafe' as it began to rain harder.

'Fancy a cappuccino, Scarlet?' I asked her.
'Yes that would be nice, but just wait a minute...' she said, pausing and looking into my eyes.
'This is what I wanted to tell you...' as she leaned forward and kissed my mouth.
I felt her body heave as I kissed her lips. She pushed herself towards me and held me tight.
'You know Markus, when I first set eyes on you I

The Master of the Cube

knew you were the one, and I'm not kidding either' she said.
'The feeling is mutual, Scarlet' I said, again kissing her lips.
'Come on, let's go inside' I said.
'You'll get cold out here' I said, opening the door for her into the Cafe.

Mandy's Cafe was my regular. I had spent a lot of time in there, and as we walked in the jukebox was blasting out Rock 'n' Roll tunes. She noticed pictures of the most recent and past film stars hung artistically all over the walls.
'What a lovely Cafe' thought Scarlet, taking a pew at the bar as I joined her.

'Hi, two cappuccinos please' I asked.
The woman behind the bar made up two cappuccinos as the sound of the squirting coffee maker echoed throughout the Cafe. Chinking cutlery, laughter and the delightful Rock 'n' Roll tunes resonated throughout this wonderful place as the woman placed the mugs on the bar.

'So what made you want to be in my film?' I asked her curiously.
'I loved the other three. I have always wanted to be a film idol' she said taking a sip from her mug.
'I like romantic men...That's why I like you Markus, you come across as a sensitive and kind soul,' she said with a smile.
'I have to admit, I don't like that Rock 'n' Roll guy though, he really gets on my nerves' she said with a slight frown.

'Yes, don't worry about him, he does that to all the ladies. I find him an egotistical bogus bum head, to be honest' I said.
She laughed...
'What made you want to have your hair that way?' she asked, running her fingers through my scalp.
'I don't really know...I just like it I guess' I said.
'It's lovely' she said.
'Is that natural blond?' she asked.
'Yes, it is' I replied with a smile.
'Do you know what I'd like to do for you most?' I asked her.
'No,' she replied.
'I'd like to build you a castle on top of a hill and we could stay there forever...' I said, kissing her on the lips.
She laughed and blushed...
'I would like that...' she smiled.
'I would shower you with gifts and roses every day...I really mean it' I said.
She blushed...
'Are you seeing anyone Markus? Don't worry, I can take it' she said.
'Yes...her name is Cynthia but she is rather bland compared to you to be honest' I said, placing my hand on my chin.
She smiled...
'My man is a nut. He would go crazy if knew about this...no exaggeration' she said quietly.
'David...he's a bastard, that's for sure. I can't wait to leave him, but he scares me' she said, taking another sip from her hot frothy drink.
'Why do you stick with him then?' I asked, concerned.

The Master of the Cube

'Like I said he's a bastard, he hits me sometimes' she said.
'Oh gosh, that's no good' I said.
'You can't let him rule you like that' I said, holding her hand softly.
'You stick with me, you'll be fine, I promise' I said.
'He doesn't deserve you, men like that don't appreciate a nice lady like you' I said calmly,
'I won't hit you, I am a loving man' I said.
'I know, that's why I want you so badly Markus' she said.
'Look...David's away on business for a few days; do you want to come back to my apartment?' she said politely.
'Yes, I would like that, my car is around the back of the Cafe' I said as we grabbed our coats and rushed to the car in the pouring rain.

Back at Scarlet's apartment...

Scarlet's apartment was really nice, tidy, clean with a large tan square shaped leather sofa. A tiger skin rug was in the centre of the room and a large but stylish coffee table sat opposite the sofa. A rather nice looking bar was in the corner with all the spirits you could think of with a bar butler running across the top. There were two large glass sliding doors at the back which opened out on a balcony which looked over the town. Scarlet poured me a drink and we opened the doors and stood on the balcony and looked over the town. I could see the headlamps of the cars going about their business below and I could also see the large Hollywood sign on the hill in the distance. It had stopped raining, just a trickle of residue was left on the roads and the moon had made an appearance. We stood holding our cocktail glasses and held each other tight under a killing moon...wishing upon a star...

'Do you like it here Markus?' she asked.
'Yes I love it, I like your apartment' I said.
'It's really lovely' I said, looking back into the apartment,
'Are you sure David won't come home?' I asked her.
'Yes, don't worry he's in New York on business' she said, placing her hand on my buttocks, and running her fingers around the rim of her glass.

'Come on, follow me...this way' she said grabbing my hand and pulling me towards the bedroom.

I followed her, feeling very excited. She sat me on the bed and slowly unbuttoned her white dress from the front and revealed her lovely breasts. She was beautiful, tall and slender. She let her dress drop to her ankles exposing her long legs. She slowly took of her red high heeled shoes and threw them on the bedroom floor, tossed her hair back and thrust her chest deep into my face. I frantically undressed; she unbuttoned my white shirt and she ran her nails along the fine hairs on my chest which sent little ripples of excitement tingling down my abdomen. She wrapped her legs tight around my body, leaning her head and chest backwards towards the floor, as I thrust my pelvis deep inside her.

The Master of the Cube

Suddenly there was a loud crash, and the doors to the apartment flew open!
'YOU CHEATING BITCH!' the man shouted.
'I KNEW IT!' screamed David.
'NO DAVID!' yelled Scarlett, edging back towards the wall.
'WHO THE HELL'S THIS?' shouted David.

David was tall, built like a 'brick shit house' and very smartly dressed. I could see the anger in his eyes which bulged with hatred as he stared sternly at me, which unsettled me greatly.

'Look, I don't want any trouble' I said calmly.
'MESSING ABOUT WITH MY GIRL, HEY!' shouted David and he punched me hard in the face as I fell to the floor. Blood descended from the corner of my mouth.
'YOU'LL PAY FOR THIS!' he said, punching me again.
'NO DAVID, DON'T HURT HIM!' screamed Scarlett in floods of hysterical tears.
'GET OUT!' David shouted, throwing me and my clothes into the outside of the apartment.
David slammed the door shut...I could hear David slapping her hard as she screamed out,
which was a horrible affair.
'What an animal!' I thought.

A few hours later...

I entered my front door.
'Where the hell have you been?' asked Cynthia, concerned.

'I got held up' I said.
'Hey what's that on your face? That's blood isn't it?' asked Cynthia.
'What the hell happened?' she asked concerned.
'Some guys in the café beat the fuck out of me!' I exclaimed.
'What…?' said Cynthia.
'Are you alright?' she asked, placing her hand on my back.
'Yes I'll be fine, I just want to get cleaned up that's all' I said.
'Who were these guys?' asked Cynthia.
'Teddy boys' I replied, feeling guilty as I knew I was lying.

I went to bed…

The next day…

I went to the set eager to see Scarlet. I was apprehensive for her, knowing that I had left her with that animal. I scanned the set, but there was no sign of Scarlet. 'Where is she?' I thought.
'God, I hope she's alright' I thought, concerned.
The minutes ticked by.
'Where the hell is Scarlet?' exclaimed Jonathan.
'We bloody well need her here' he said.
The hours passed…

'Damn Scarlet! We will have to look for a replacement, I'm not having this' said Jonathan in a forceful tone.
'We will have to pack up for today. Joseph, get on to the agency and find a replacement quick, got it!'

snapped the director.

What a bastard I thought Jonathan was at that moment. He had let us down, no one could match Scarlet's charm, I thought, disgruntled.

Later that evening…

Scarlet sat on the edge of the bed. There were bruises on her face and a whopping shiner from David who had gone ballistic when he found out that she had being seeing another man.
The phone suddenly rang…

She answered…

'Scarlet, where the hell were you today?' asked Jonathan.
'I waited four hours for you to show, what the hell's going on?' he asked.
'Well…?' he said

Scarlet was too cut up to speak…

'Sod you!' he said. 'You'll never make it as a film star honey!' he snapped and very unreasonably slammed down the phone…

Scarlet had fallen into a great depression. She was hurt and upset and her self esteem had really sunk.
'I'm finished' she thought, reaching for the sleeping tablets…

The next day Scarlet was found dead in her

apartment. She had taken an overdose…

The tragic part of the story was a letter was in the post to Scarlet offering her a major role in a Hollywood blockbuster…

How heartbreaking…

She was beautiful, I had her and then she was gone…my little angel.

She broke my heart…

www.ingramcontent.com/pod-product-compliance
Ingram Content Group UK Ltd.
Pitfield, Milton Keynes, MK11 3LW, UK
UKHW041412180426
11947UKWH00007B/95